The Cure for Evil Eye & Envy

THE ISLAMIC APPROACH

The Cure for Evil Eye & Envy

THE ISLAMIC APPROACH

1 2 3 4 5 6 7 8 9 10

All rights reserved. No part of this publication may be reproduced, stored in a retrieval system or transmitted in any form or by any means – electronic, mechanical, photocopying, recording or otherwise – without written permission from the publisher.

© Light Publishing 2024

Shaykh Khālid bin ʿIbrāhīm al-Ḥibshī

The Cure For Evil Eye & Envy

ISBN 978-1-915570-62-8

www.lightpublishing.co.uk

بسم الله الرحمن الرحيم

CONTENTS

INTRODUCTION	9
Signs & Indications for the Affliction of Evil Eye & Envy	11
Treatment for the Evil Eye & Envy	13
The Verses of Ruqya for Evil Eye & Envy	15
Ruqyah Through Supplications	31
Treatments Permitted to be Utilized as a Supplement with Ruqyah	37
Advice for Women	39
Advice for men	43
Tools Utilized as Ornaments Falsely Believing That They Repel Evil Eye & Envy	45
Legal Verdict [*Fatwā*] About Aromatherapy	47

INTRODUCTION

For Evil Eye and envy is an exceptional strength that a majority of people do not believe in, such that it could demolish a mountain. The Messenger of Allah ﷺ said:

«العَيْنُ حَقٌّ، تَسْتَنْزِلُ الْحَالِقَ».

"The Evil Eye is true; it can topple al-Ḥāliq," in other words, it can topple the towering mountain. (Ṣaḥīḥ al-Jāmiʿ #4146)

The Evil Eye can affect the intellect, provision, beauty, religion, character, marriage and family life, life in general, physical health, creatures and vegetation, work, and knowledge, among other areas.

Shaykh Khālid bin
'Ibrāhīm al-Ḥibshī

SIGNS & INDICATIONS FOR THE AFFLICTION OF EVIL EYE & ENVY

Among the signs and indications are: persistent yawning without sleepiness; excessive burping despite not eating and even more so upon recitation of the Quran; scratching (itching); the appearance of pustules and boils; feeling hot or cold without reason; tightness in the chest; drowsiness, laziness, and insomnia; whispers; bloating of the body (obesity) despite eating very little; some cases of cancer; some mental illness cases like dementia and delusions; forgetfulness; hair-loss; blackness under the eyes and paleness in the face despite a lack of exertion; persistent headache; the appearance of spots under the skin like bruises that are the color of coffee beans or blue, specifically in the area of the thighs or arms; pain in the esophagus and upper-stomach that doctors cannot resolve; desire to leave home and a dislike to remain there; feeling of impending death and despair; visions of deceased persons or geckos in dreams; to be stricken with different severe illnesses that change location [in the body] which medicine cannot identify- the results come back "healthy" despite the presence of pain; a lack of response to the best of medications in the body of the sick person [suffering] from an organic sickness and this, even if the dosages are increased; the appearance of ants in the home, and the correct opinion is that of small ants- they appear despite the lack of any holes for them to come from and they are noticeable due to their great number; infants crying a great deal; visions of some perpetrators of Evil Eye from among the sick person's close friends or relatives in dreams- they look at the sick person with malicious stares or the sick person hears them speak about him and he sees their eyes in an ugly way ... etc.

TREATMENT FOR THE EVIL EYE & ENVY

First: when the perpetrator of Evil Eye is known-
From the Sunnah is what Aa'ishah ﷺ said: the perpetrator of Evil Eye would be ordered to make minor ablution, then the one afflicted would make major ablution with [the water of ablution]; and this is the best of the ways. There are similar ways like taking something from among the clothing of the perpetrator of Evil Eye, something that would contain some of his sweat or saliva (a head covering, t-shirt, shirt, left -over drink); submerge the article in water and then make major ablution with that water.

Second: when the perpetrator of Evil Eye is not known-
In this case, the remedy is through legislated Ruqyah and permissible treatments transmitted in narrations of the Messenger of Allah ﷺ. Also [permitted] is anything whose testing has been conducted and a benefit is found in it as long as its origin is permissible.

THE VERSES OF RUQYAH FOR EVIL EYE & ENVY

This is an abbreviated mention for some of the verses in which there is benefit and healing that the one afflicted by Evil Eye can recite upon himself, as well as over water, olive oil and honey.

1) Al-Fātiḥah

بِسْمِ اللَّهِ الرَّحْمَنِ الرَّحِيمِ
الْحَمْدُ لِلَّهِ رَبِّ الْعَالَمِينَ
الرَّحْمَنِ الرَّحِيمِ
مَالِكِ يَوْمِ الدِّينِ
إِيَّاكَ نَعْبُدُ وَإِيَّاكَ نَسْتَعِينُ
اهْدِنَا الصِّرَاطَ الْمُسْتَقِيمَ
صِرَاطَ الَّذِينَ أَنْعَمْتَ عَلَيْهِمْ غَيْرِ الْمَغْضُوبِ عَلَيْهِمْ وَلاَ الضَّالِّينَ

"I seek refuge in Allah from the accursed Satan "In the name of Allah, the Beneficent, the Merciful. *All the praises and thanks be to Allah, the Lord of the 'Âlamîn (mankind, jinn and all that exists) *The Most Gracious, the Most Merciful. *The Only Owner (and the Only Ruling Judge) of the Day of

Recompense (i.e. the Day of Resurrection). *You (Alone) we worship, and You (Alone) we ask for help (for each and everything). *Guide us to the Straight Way. *The Way of those on whom You have bestowed Your Grace, not (the way) of those who earned Your Anger (such as the Jews), nor of those who went astray (such as the Christians)."

2) Al-Baqarah: verse 7

«خَتَمَ اللَّهُ عَلَىٰ قُلُوبِهِمْ وَعَلَىٰ سَمْعِهِمْ وَعَلَىٰ أَبْصَارِهِمْ غِشَاوَةٌ وَلَهُمْ عَذَابٌ عَظِيمٌ».

"Allâh has set a seal on their hearts and on their hearings, and on their eyes there is a covering. Theirs will be a great torment."

3) Al-Baqarah: verse 20

«يَكَادُ الْبَرْقُ يَخْطَفُ أَبْصَارَهُمْ كُلَّمَا أَضَاءَ لَهُم مَّشَوْا فِيهِ وَإِذَا أَظْلَمَ عَلَيْهِمْ قَامُوا وَلَوْ شَاءَ اللَّهُ لَذَهَبَ بِسَمْعِهِمْ وَأَبْصَارِهِمْ إِنَّ اللَّهَ عَلَىٰ كُلِّ شَيْءٍ قَدِيرٌ».

"The lightning almost snatches away their sight, whenever it flashes for them, they walk therein, and when darkness covers them, they stand still. And if Allâh willed, He could have taken away their hearing and their sight. Certainly, Allâh has power over all things."

4) Al-Baqarah: verse 55

«وَإِذْ قُلْتُمْ يَا مُوسَىٰ لَن نُّؤْمِنَ لَكَ حَتَّىٰ نَرَى اللَّهَ جَهْرَةً فَأَخَذَتْكُمُ الصَّاعِقَةُ وَأَنتُمْ تَنظُرُونَ».

"And (remember) when you said: "O Mûsa (Moses)! We shall never believe in you till we see Allâh plainly." But you were seized with a thunderbolt (lightning) while you were looking."

5) Al-Baqarah: verse 105

«مَا يَوَدُّ الَّذِينَ كَفَرُوا مِنْ أَهْلِ الْكِتَابِ وَلَا الْمُشْرِكِينَ أَنْ يُنَزَّلَ عَلَيْكُمْ مِنْ خَيْرٍ مِنْ رَبِّكُمْ وَاللَّهُ يَخْتَصُّ بِرَحْمَتِهِ مَنْ يَشَاءُ وَاللَّهُ ذُو الْفَضْلِ الْعَظِيمِ».

"Neither those who disbelieve among the people of the Scripture (Jews and Christians) nor Al-Mushrikûn like that there should be sent down unto you any good from your Lord. But Allâh chooses for His Mercy whom He wills. And Allâh is the Owner of Great Bounty."

6) Al-Baqarah: verse 109

«وَدَّ كَثِيرٌ مِّنْ أَهْلِ ٱلْكِتَٰبِ لَوْ يَرُدُّونَكُم مِّن بَعْدِ إِيمَٰنِكُمْ كُفَّارًا حَسَدًا مِّنْ عِندِ أَنفُسِهِم مِّنۢ بَعْدِ مَا تَبَيَّنَ لَهُمُ ٱلْحَقُّ فَٱعْفُوا۟ وَٱصْفَحُوا۟ حَتَّىٰ يَأْتِيَ ٱللَّهُ بِأَمْرِهِ إِنَّ ٱللَّهَ عَلَىٰ كُلِّ شَىْءٍ قَدِيرٌ».

"Many of the people of the Scripture (Jews and Christians) wish that if they could turn you away as disbelievers aft er you have believed, out of envy from their ownselves, even aft er the truth has become manifest unto them. But forgive and overlook, till Allâh brings His Command. Verily, Allâh is Abl to do all things."

7) Al-Baqarah: verse 247

»وَقَالَ لَهُمْ نَبِيُّهُمْ إِنَّ اللَّهَ قَدْ بَعَثَ لَكُمْ طَالُوتَ مَلِكًا قَالُوا أَنَّىٰ يَكُونُ لَهُ الْمُلْكُ عَلَيْنَا وَنَحْنُ أَحَقُّ بِالْمُلْكِ مِنْهُ وَلَمْ يُؤْتَ سَعَةً مِنَ الْمَالِ قَالَ إِنَّ اللَّهَ اصْطَفَاهُ عَلَيْكُمْ وَزَادَهُ بَسْطَةً فِي الْعِلْمِ وَالْجِسْمِ وَاللَّهُ يُؤْتِي مُلْكَهُ مَن يَشَاءُ وَاللَّهُ وَاسِعٌ عَلِيمٌ«.

"And their Prophet (Samuel ﷺ) said to them, "Indeed Allâh has appointed Talût (Saul) as a king over you." They said, "How can he be a king over us when we are fitter than him for the kingdom, and he has not been given enough wealth." He said: "Verily, Allâh has chosen him above you and has increased him abundantly in knowledge and stature. And Allâh grants His Kingdom to whom He wills. And Allâh is All-Sufficient for His creatures' needs, All-Knower.""

8) Al-Baqarah: verse 255

» اللَّهُ لَا إِلَٰهَ إِلَّا هُوَ الْحَيُّ الْقَيُّومُ لَا تَأْخُذُهُ سِنَةٌ وَلَا نَوْمٌ لَّهُ مَا فِي السَّمَاوَاتِ وَمَا فِي الْأَرْضِ مَن ذَا الَّذِي يَشْفَعُ عِندَهُ إِلَّا بِإِذْنِهِ

«يَعْلَمُ مَا بَيْنَ أَيْدِيهِمْ وَمَا خَلْفَهُمْ وَلَا يُحِيطُونَ بِشَيْءٍ مِنْ عِلْمِهِ إِلَّا بِمَا شَاءَ وَسِعَ كُرْسِيُّهُ السَّمَاوَاتِ وَالْأَرْضَ وَلَا يَؤُودُهُ حِفْظُهُمَا وَهُوَ الْعَلِيُّ الْعَظِيمُ».

"Allâh! Lâ ilâha illa Huwa (none has the right to be worshipped but He), the Ever Living, the One Who sustains and protects all that exists. Neither slumber, nor sleep overtake Him. To Him belongs whatever is in the heavens and whatever is on earth. Who is he that can intercede with Him except with His Permission? He knows what happens to them (His creatures) in this world, and what will happen to them in the Hereafter. And they will never compass anything of His Knowledge except that which He wills. His Kursî extends over the heavens and the earth, and He feels no fatigue in guarding and preserving them. And He is the Most High, the Most Great. [This Verse 2:255 is called Ayat-ul-Kursî.]"

9) Al-Baqarah: verse 269

«يُؤْتِي الْحِكْمَةَ مَنْ يَشَاءُ وَمَنْ يُؤْتَ الْحِكْمَةَ فَقَدْ أُوتِيَ خَيْرًا كَثِيرًا وَمَا يَذَّكَّرُ إِلَّا أُولُو الْأَلْبَابِ».

"He grants Hikmah to whom He pleases, and he, to whom Hikmah is granted, is indeed granted abundant good. But none remember (will receive admonition) except men of understanding."

10) Al-Baqarah: verses 285-286

«آمَنَ الرَّسُولُ بِمَا أُنزِلَ إِلَيْهِ مِن رَّبِّهِ وَالْمُؤْمِنُونَ كُلٌّ آمَنَ بِاللَّهِ وَمَلَائِكَتِهِ وَكُتُبِهِ وَرُسُلِهِ لَا نُفَرِّقُ بَيْنَ أَحَدٍ مِّن رُّسُلِهِ وَقَالُوا سَمِعْنَا وَأَطَعْنَا غُفْرَانَكَ رَبَّنَا وَإِلَيْكَ الْمَصِيرُ ﴿285﴾ لَا يُكَلِّفُ اللَّهُ نَفْسًا إِلَّا وُسْعَهَا لَهَا مَا كَسَبَتْ وَعَلَيْهَا مَا اكْتَسَبَتْ رَبَّنَا لَا تُؤَاخِذْنَا إِن نَّسِينَا أَوْ أَخْطَأْنَا رَبَّنَا وَلَا تَحْمِلْ عَلَيْنَا إِصْرًا كَمَا حَمَلْتَهُ عَلَى الَّذِينَ مِن قَبْلِنَا رَبَّنَا وَلَا تُحَمِّلْنَا مَا لَا طَاقَةَ لَنَا بِهِ وَاعْفُ عَنَّا وَاغْفِرْ لَنَا وَارْحَمْنَا أَنتَ مَوْلَانَا فَانصُرْنَا عَلَى الْقَوْمِ الْكَافِرِينَ».

"The Messenger (Muhammad ﷺ) believes in what has been sent down to him from his Lord, and (so do) the believers. Each one believes in Allâh, His Angels, His Books, and His Messengers. (They say), "We make no distinction between one another of His Messengers" and they say, "We hear, and we obey. (We seek) Your Forgiveness, our Lord, and to You is the return (of all)." (285) Allâh burdens not a person beyond his scope. He gets reward for that (good) which he has earned, and he is punished for that (evil) which he has earned. "Our Lord! Punish us not if we forget or fall into error, our Lord! Lay not on us a burden like that which You did lay on those before us (Jews and Christians); our Lord! Put not on us a burden greater than we have strength to bear. Pardon us and grant us Forgiveness. Have mercy on us. You are our Maulâ (Patron, Supporter and Protector, etc.) and give us victory over the disbelieving people.""

11) An-Nisā': verse 32

«وَلَا تَتَمَنَّوْا مَا فَضَّلَ اللَّهُ بِهِ بَعْضَكُمْ عَلَىٰ بَعْضٍ لِّلرِّجَالِ نَصِيبٌ مِّمَّا اكْتَسَبُوا وَلِلنِّسَاءِ نَصِيبٌ مِّمَّا اكْتَسَبْنَ وَاسْأَلُوا اللَّهَ مِن فَضْلِهِ إِنَّ اللَّهَ كَانَ بِكُلِّ شَيْءٍ عَلِيمًا».

"And wish not for the things in which Allâh has made some of you to excel others. For men there is reward for what they have earned, (and likewise) for women there is reward for what they have earned, and ask Allâh of His Bounty. Surely, Allâh is Ever All-Knower of everything."

12) An-Nisā': verse 54

«أَمْ يَحْسُدُونَ النَّاسَ عَلَىٰ مَا آتَاهُمُ اللَّهُ مِن فَضْلِهِ فَقَدْ آتَيْنَا آلَ إِبْرَاهِيمَ الْكِتَابَ وَالْحِكْمَةَ وَآتَيْنَاهُم مُّلْكًا عَظِيمًا».

"Or do they envy men (Muhammad ﷺ and his followers) for what Allâh has given them of His Bounty? Then We had already given the family of Ibrâhim (Abraham) the Book and Al-Hikmah (As-Sunnah - Divine Revelation to those Prophets not written in the form of a book), and conferred upon them a great kingdom."

13) Al-'An`ām: verse 53

«وَكَذَلِكَ فَتَنَّا بَعْضَهُم بِبَعْضٍ لِيَقُولُوا أَهَٰؤُلَاءِ مَنَّ اللَّهُ عَلَيْهِم مِّن بَيْنِنَا أَلَيْسَ اللَّهُ بِأَعْلَمَ بِالشَّاكِرِينَ».

"Thus We have tried some of them with others, that they might say: "Is it these (poor believers) that Allâh has favoured from amongst us?" Does not Allâh know best those who are grateful?"

14) Yūnus: verse 43

«وَمِنْهُم مَّن يَنظُرُ إِلَيْكَ أَفَأَنتَ تَهْدِي الْعُمْيَ وَلَوْ كَانُوا لَا يُبْصِرُونَ».

"And among them are some who look at you, but can you guide the blind, even though they see not?"

15) Yūsuf: verse 5

«قَالَ يَا بُنَيَّ لَا تَقْصُصْ رُؤْيَاكَ عَلَىٰ إِخْوَتِكَ فَيَكِيدُوا لَكَ كَيْدًا إِنَّ الشَّيْطَانَ لِلْإِنسَانِ عَدُوٌّ مُّبِينٌ».

"He (the father) said: "O my son! Relate not your vision to your brothers, lest they arrange a plot against you. Verily! Shaitân (Satan) is to man an open enemy!"

16) Yūsuf: verse 31

«فَلَمَّا سَمِعَتْ بِمَكْرِهِنَّ أَرْسَلَتْ إِلَيْهِنَّ وَأَعْتَدَتْ لَهُنَّ مُتَّكَأً وَآتَتْ كُلَّ

وَاحِدَةٍ مِنْهُنَّ سِكِّينًا وَقَالَتِ اخْرُجْ عَلَيْهِنَّ فَلَمَّا رَأَيْنَهُ أَكْبَرْنَهُ وَقَطَّعْنَ أَيْدِيَهُنَّ وَقُلْنَ حَاشَ لِلَّهِ مَا هَذَا بَشَرًا إِنْ هَذَا إِلَّا مَلَكٌ كَرِيمٌ».

"So when she heard of their accusati on, she sent for them and prepared a banquet for them; she gave each one of them a knife (to cut the foodstuff with), and she said [(to Yûsuf (Joseph)]: "Come out before them." Then, when they saw him, they exalted him (at his beauty) and (in their astonishment) cut their hands. They said: "How perfect is Allâh (or Allâh forbid)! No man is this! This is none other than a noble angel!"

17) Yūsuf: verse 56

«وَكَذَلِكَ مَكَّنَّا لِيُوسُفَ فِي الْأَرْضِ يَتَبَوَّأُ مِنْهَا حَيْثُ يَشَاءُ نُصِيبُ بِرَحْمَتِنَا مَنْ نَشَاءُ وَلَا نُضِيعُ أَجْرَ الْمُحْسِنِينَ».

"Thus did We give full authority to Yûsuf (Joseph) in the land, to take possession therein, when or where he likes. We bestow of Our Mercy on whom We will, and We make not to be lost the reward of Al-Muhsinûn."

18) Yūsuf: verses 67-68

«وَقَالَ يَا بَنِيَّ لَا تَدْخُلُوا مِنْ بَابٍ وَاحِدٍ وَادْخُلُوا مِنْ أَبْوَابٍ مُتَفَرِّقَةٍ وَمَا أُغْنِي عَنْكُمْ مِنَ اللَّهِ مِنْ شَيْءٍ إِنِ الْحُكْمُ إِلَّا لِلَّهِ عَلَيْهِ تَوَكَّلْتُ وَعَلَيْهِ فَلْيَتَوَكَّلِ الْمُتَوَكِّلُونَ ﴿67﴾ وَلَمَّا دَخَلُوا مِنْ حَيْثُ أَمَرَهُمْ أَبُوهُمْ مَا كَانَ يُغْنِي عَنْهُمْ مِنَ اللَّهِ مِنْ شَيْءٍ إِلَّا

THE CURE FOR EVIL EYE & ENVY

»حَاجَةً فِي نَفْسِ يَعْقُوبَ قَضَاهَا وَإِنَّهُ لَذُو عِلْمٍ لِمَا عَلَّمْنَاهُ وَلَكِنَّ أَكْثَرَ النَّاسِ لَا يَعْلَمُونَ«.

"And he said: "O my sons! Do not enter by one gate, but enter by different gates, and I cannot avail you against Allâh at all. Verily! The decision rests only with Allâh. In him, I put my trust and let all those that trust, put their trust in Him." (67) And when they entered according to their father's advice, it did not avail them in the least against (the Will of) Allâh, it was but a need of Ya'qûb's (Jacob) inner-self which he discharged. And verily, he was endowed with knowledge because We had taught him, but most men know not."

19) Al-Ḥijr: verse 88

»لَا تَمُدَّنَّ عَيْنَيْكَ إِلَى مَا مَتَّعْنَا بِهِ أَزْوَاجًا مِنْهُمْ وَلَا تَحْزَنْ عَلَيْهِمْ وَاخْفِضْ جَنَاحَكَ لِلْمُؤْمِنِينَ«.

"Look not with your eyes ambitiously at what We have bestowed on certain classes of them (the disbelievers), nor grieve over them. And lower your wings for the believers (be courteous to the fellow-believers)."

20) Al-Kahf: verse 39

»وَلَوْلَا إِذْ دَخَلْتَ جَنَّتَكَ قُلْتَ مَا شَاءَ اللَّهُ لَا قُوَّةَ إِلَّا بِاللَّهِ إِنْ تَرَنِ أَنَا أَقَلَّ مِنْكَ مَالًا وَوَلَدًا«.

"It was better for you to say, when you entered your garden: 'That which Allâh wills (will come to pass)! There is no power but with Allâh'. If you see me less than you in wealth, and children."

21) An-Naml: verse 15

«وَلَقَدْ آتَيْنَا دَاوُودَ وَسُلَيْمَانَ عِلْمًا وَقَالَا الْحَمْدُ لِلَّهِ الَّذِي فَضَّلَنَا عَلَى كَثِيرٍ مِنْ عِبَادِهِ الْمُؤْمِنِينَ».

"And indeed We gave knowledge to Dawûd (David) and Sulaimân (Solomon), and they both said: "All the praises and thanks are to Allâh, Who has preferred us above many of His believing slaves!""

22) Al-Qaṣaṣ: verse 79

«فَخَرَجَ عَلَى قَوْمِهِ فِي زِينَتِهِ قَالَ الَّذِينَ يُرِيدُونَ الْحَيَاةَ الدُّنْيَا يَا لَيْتَ لَنَا مِثْلَ مَا أُوتِيَ قَارُونُ إِنَّهُ لَذُو حَظٍّ عَظِيمٍ».

"So he went forth before his people in his pomp. Those who were desirous of the life of the world, said: "Ah, would that we had the like of what Qârûn (Korah) has been given! Verily, he is the owner of a great fortune.""

23) YāSīn: verse 66

«وَلَوْ نَشَاءُ لَطَمَسْنَا عَلَى أَعْيُنِهِمْ فَاسْتَبَقُوا الصِّرَاطَ فَأَنَّى يُبْصِرُونَ».

"And if it had been Our Will, We would surely have wiped out (blinded) their eyes, so that they would struggle for the Path, how then would they see?"

24) Ghāfir: verse 19

«يَعْلَمُ خَائِنَةَ الْأَعْيُنِ وَمَا تُخْفِي الصُّدُورُ».

"Allâh knows the fraud of the eyes, and all that the breasts conceal."

25) Muḥammad: verses 29-30

«أَمْ حَسِبَ الَّذِينَ فِي قُلُوبِهِمْ مَرَضٌ أَنْ لَنْ يُخْرِجَ اللَّهُ أَضْغَانَهُمْ ﴿29﴾ وَلَوْ نَشَاءُ لَأَرَيْنَاكَهُمْ فَلَعَرَفْتَهُمْ بِسِيمَاهُمْ وَلَتَعْرِفَنَّهُمْ فِي لَحْنِ الْقَوْلِ وَاللَّهُ يَعْلَمُ أَعْمَالَكُمْ».

"Or do those in whose hearts is a disease (of hypocrisy), think that Allâh will not bring to light all their hidden ill-wills? (29) Had We willed, We could have shown them to you, and you should have known them by their marks; but surely, you will know them by the tone of their speech! And Allâh knows (all) your deeds."

26) Al-Fat'ḥ: verse 15

«سَيَقُولُ الْمُخَلَّفُونَ إِذَا انْطَلَقْتُمْ إِلَى مَغَانِمَ لِتَأْخُذُوهَا ذَرُونَا نَتَّبِعْكُمْ يُرِيدُونَ أَنْ يُبَدِّلُوا كَلَامَ اللَّهِ قُلْ لَنْ تَتَّبِعُونَا كَذَلِكُمْ قَالَ اللَّهُ مِنْ

«قَبْلُ فَسَيَقُولُونَ بَلْ تَحْسُدُونَنَا بَلْ كَانُوا لَا يَفْقَهُونَ إِلَّا قَلِيلًا».

"Those who lagged behind will say, when you set forth to take the spoils, "Allow us to follow you," They want to change Allâh's Words. Say: "You shall not follow us; thus Allâh has said beforehand." Then they will say: "Nay, you envy us." Nay, but they understand not except a little."

27) Al-Mumtaḥinah: verse 2

«إِنْ يَثْقَفُوكُمْ يَكُونُوا لَكُمْ أَعْدَاءً وَيَبْسُطُوا إِلَيْكُمْ أَيْدِيَهُمْ وَأَلْسِنَتَهُمْ بِالسُّوءِ وَوَدُّوا لَوْ تَكْفُرُونَ».

"Should they gain the upper hand over you, they would behave to you as enemies, and stretch forth their hands and their tongues against you with evil, and they desire that you should disbelieve."

28) Al-Mulk: verses 2-3

«الَّذِي خَلَقَ الْمَوْتَ وَالْحَيَاةَ لِيَبْلُوَكُمْ أَيُّكُمْ أَحْسَنُ عَمَلًا وَهُوَ الْعَزِيزُ الْغَفُورُ ﴿2﴾ الَّذِي خَلَقَ سَبْعَ سَمَاوَاتٍ طِبَاقًا مَا تَرَىٰ فِي خَلْقِ الرَّحْمَٰنِ مِنْ تَفَاوُتٍ فَارْجِعِ الْبَصَرَ هَلْ تَرَىٰ مِنْ فُطُورٍ».

"Who has created the seven heavens one above another, you can see no fault in the creation of the Most Gracious. Then look again: "Can you see any rift s?" (3) Then look again and yet again, your sight will return to you in a state of humiliation and worn out."

29) Al-Qalam: verses 51-52

«وَإِن يَكَادُ الَّذِينَ كَفَرُوا لَيُزْلِقُونَكَ بِأَبْصَارِهِمْ لَمَّا سَمِعُوا الذِّكْرَ وَيَقُولُونَ إِنَّهُ لَمَجْنُونٌ ﴿51﴾ وَمَا هُوَ إِلَّا ذِكْرٌ لِلْعَالَمِينَ».

"And verily, those who disbelieve would almost make you slip with their eyes (through hatred) when they hear the Reminder (the Qur'ân), and they say: "Verily, he (Muhammad ﷺ) is a madman!" (51) But it is nothing else than a Reminder to all the 'Alamîn (mankind, jinn and all that exists)."

30) Al-Kawthar, Al-Kāfirūn, Al-'Ikhlāṣ, Al-Falaq, and An-Nās

Recite this Ruqyah with concentration on the meaning of the verses, then make note of any indications the sick person encounters, for example: feeling hot or cold coming from his extremities; headaches or dizziness; lethargy, drowsiness, and sleepiness; needle pricks on the body; nausea; pain in the shoulders; something like ants crawling along the back; sweating; rapid heartbeat, etc. If these symptoms are found, repeat the Ruqyah as many times as possible, three or more times; or, when the sick person feels that a specific verse is having an effect, then it should be repeated a great deal without limiting the number of times. There are six verses for healing, verses for tranquility, and verses for every affliction. There are verses of knowledge for someone afflicted regarding his intelligence; verses of beauty, provision and similar things.

There are also supplications, some of which, Ibn al-Qayyim mentioned.

RUQYAH THROUGH SUPPLICATIONS

1) Ṣaḥīḥ Muslim #2708

«أَعُوذُ بِكَلِمَاتِ اللهِ التَّامَّاتِ مِنْ شَرِّ مَا خَلَقَ».

"I seek refuge in the perfect words of Allah from the evil that He created."

2) Ṣaḥīḥ al-Bukhārī #3191

«أَعُوذُ بِكَلِمَاتِ اللهِ التَّامَّةِ، مِنْ كُلِّ شَيْطَانٍ وَهَامَّةٍ، وَمِنْ كُلِّ عَيْنٍ لَامَّةٍ».

"I seek refuge in the perfect words of Allah from every Satan and pest; and from every jealous, evil eye."

3) Musnad al-'Imām 'Aḥmad #15461

«أعوذ بكلمات الله التامات التي لا يجاوزهن برٌّ ولا فاجرٌ من شرِّ ما خلق وذرأ وبرأ ومن شرِّ ما ينزلُ من السماء ومن شرِّ ما يعرجُ فيها ومن شرِّ ما ذرأ في الأرض وما يخرجُ منها ومن شرِّ فتنِ الليلِ والنهارِ ومن شرِّ كلِّ طارقٍ إلا طارقًا يطرقُ بخيرٍ يا رحمنُ».

"I seek refuge in the perfect words of Allah- which no one, whether righteous or wicked, can surpass- from the evil of what He created, spread [throughout time and creation] and free [of disproportion]; from the evil He sent down from the sky; from the evil that ascends to it; from the evil that He created in the earth; from the evil that comes out of it; from the evil of the trials of day and night; from the evil of the paths of the night except the one tread with good, Oh Most Merciful!"

4) Aṭ-Ṭibb an-Nabawī p. 125

«تحصّنتُ بالذي لا إلهَ إلَّا هو إلهي وإلهُ كلِّ شيءٍ واعتصمتُ بربّي وبربُّ كلِّ شيءٍ وتوكلتُ على الحيِّ الذي لا يموتُ واستدفعتُ الشرَّ بلا حولَ ولا قوةَ إلَّا بالله، حسبيَ اللهُ ونعمَ الوكيلُ، حسبيَ الربُّ من العباد، حسبيَ الخالقُ من المخلوقِ، حسبيَ الرزاقُ من المرزوقِ، حسبيَ الذي هو حسبي، حسبيَ الذي بيده ملكوتُ كلِّ شيءٍ، وهو يجيرُ ولا يجارُ عليه، حسبيَ اللهُ وكفَى، سمعَ اللهُ لمن دعا، ليس وراءَ اللهِ مَرمَى، حسبيَ اللهُ لا إلهَ إلَّا هو عليه توكلتُ وهو ربُّ العرشِ العظيمِ».

"I fortify myself with Allah who there is no god except Him; my God and the God of everything. I seek shelter in my Lord and the Lord of everything. I entrust my affairs to the Ever-Living who does not die. I seek to ward off evil with "there is no power nor might except with Allah". Allah is sufficient for me and what an excellent disposer of affairs is He! The

Lord suffices me from any need for the slaves. The Creator suffices me from any need for created things. The Provider suffices me from any need for those He provides for. He who suffices me is sufficient for me. He in whose Hands is the dominion of everything suffices me- He who grants protection and against whom there is no protection- Allah suffices and is enough for me. Allah hears whoever calls- there is nothing beyond Allah's hearing. Allah suffices me- there is no god except Him; upon Him I place my trust and He is the Lord of the Might Throne."

5) Ṣaḥīḥ Muslim #2202

«ضَعْ يَدَكَ عَلَى الَّذِي تَأَلَّمَ مِنْ جَسَدِكَ، وَقُلْ: بِاسْمِ اللهِ، ثَلَاثًا، وَقُلْ سَبْعَ مَرَّاتٍ: أَعُوذُ بِاللَّهِ وَقُدْرَتِهِ مِنْ شَرِّ مَا أَجِدُ وَأُحَاذِرُ».

The Prophet ﷺ said: "Place your hand upon the part of your body that hurts and say, "In the name of Allah", three times. And say seven times, "I seek refuge in the honor of Allah and His ability from the evil that I encounter [of pain] and guard against [out of fear]."

6) Khaythamah bin Sulaymān p. 204

«اللَّهُمَّ ذَا السُّلْطَانِ العَظِيمِ وَالمَنِّ القَدِيمِ ذَا الرَّحْمَةِ الكَرِيمِ، وَلِيَّ الكَلِمَاتِ التَّامَّاتِ وَالدَّعَوَاتِ المُسْتَجَابَاتِ عَافِ حَسَنًا وَحُسَيْنًا مِنْ أَنْفُسِ الجِنِّ وَأَعْيُنِ الإِنْسِ».

"Oh Allah! Possessor of great authority and eternal favor, possessor of the Noble Face, guardian of the perfect words and supplications which are incumbent upon You to respond to- protect us from the spirits of Jinn and the eyes of human beings."

7) Ibn Mājah #3523

«بِسْمِ الله أَرْقِيكَ، مِنْ كُلِّ شَيْءٍ يُؤْذِيكَ، مِنْ شَرِّ كُلِّ نَفْسٍ أَوْ عَيْنِ حَاسِدٍ، اللهُ يَشْفِيكَ، بِسمِ اللهِ أَرْقِيكَ.»

"In the name of Allah- I perform Ruqyah for you, and may Allah cure you from everything harming you and from every Evil Eye and envy. In the name of Allah, I perform Ruqyah for you."

8) Al-Jāmi' aṣ-Ṣāghir #4571

«كلماتُ الفرج : لا إلهَ إلا اللهُ الحليمُ الكريمُ لا إلهَ إلا اللهُ العليُّ العظيمُ، لا إلهَ إلا اللهُ ربُّ السمواتِ السبعِ، و ربُّ العرشِ الكريمِ.»

"The words of relief- there is no god except Allah, the Forbearing, the Generous; there is no god except Allah, the Most Supreme, the Most Majestic; there is no god except Allah, Lord of the seven heavens and Lord of the Noble Throne."

9) Musnad al-'Imām 'Aḥmad #2137

أسألُ اللَّهَ العظيمَ، ربَّ العرشِ العظيمِ أن يشفيَك. (فيقولُهُ سَبْعَ مَرّاتٍ للمَريض)

Say for the sick person seven times: "I ask Allah, the Majestic, Lord of the Majestic Throne to heal you."

10) Al-Jāmi' aṣ-Ṣāghir #3373

لَا إِلَهَ إِلَّا أَنْتَ سُبْحَانَكَ إِنِّي كُنْتُ مِنَ الظَّالِمِينَ.
(لَمْ يَدْعُ بِهَا رَجُلٌ مُسْلِمٌ فِي شَيْءٍ إلا استجابَ لَهُ)

"There is no god except You, may You be glorified. Truly, I was one of the oppressors." A Muslim man does not supplicate for anything at all by means of this except Allah will respond to him.

11) 'Abū Dāwud #3892

«ربَّنا اللَّهُ الَّذي في السَّماءِ تقدَّسَ اسمُكَ أمرُكَ في السَّماءِ والأرضِ كما رحمتُكَ في السَّماءِ فاجعَل رحمتَكَ في الأرضِ اغفِر لَنا حوبَنا وخطايانا أنتَ ربُّ الطَّيِّبينَ أنزِل رحمةً من رحمتِكَ وشفاءً من شفائِكَ على هذا الوجَعِ فيَبرأَ».

"Our Lord is Allah who is in heaven, may Your name be sanctified. Your command is in heaven and the earth just as Your mercy is in heaven. So, make Your mercy in the earth and forgive us our sins and mistakes. You are the Lord of the Pure. Send down Your mercy and healing upon this pain so it may be cured."

TREATMENTS PERMITTED TO BE UTILIZED AS A SUPPLEMENT WITH RUQYAH

1) Zamzam Water

Drink the water of Zamzam and seek a cure by means of it as a drink, and as washing water if possible. Reciting [Ruqyah] into it is best.

2) Olive Oil

A specific use for it is to recite the Quran over it, rub the entire body with it and eat some of it as well.

3) Honey

It is a cure for people utilized in several ways- as a drink, a rub, mixture for the eyes, as well as to recite over it and use it [like olive oil].

4) Black Seed

»إنَّ هذِهِ الحَبَّةَ السَّوْدَاءَ شِفَاءٌ مِن كُلِّ دَاءٍ، إلَّا مِنَ السَّامِ«.

The Prophet ﷺ said in a narration: "Black seed is a

cure for every disease." Ṣaḥīḥ al-Bukhārī #5687 It is utilized ground-up into a powder-one teaspoon, taken twice per day; as a drink, like tea; in a vapor bath inhaled by boiling it; as a rubbing oil; as washing water with an infusion of it.

5) Infusions of Herbs
Examples are infusions like the Sidr lote-tree, sea salt, certain morning glory species, camphor, and costus.

6) Cupping
The Prophet ﷺ said: "The angel Gabriel informed me that cupping is the most beneficial treatment with which people can be treated." Ṣaḥīḥ Al-Jāmi' aṣ-Ṣaghir #218

7) There is no harm in going to someone for Ruqyah treatment however be careful of falling into the hands of a sorcerer or charlatan. Know that some claim to only treat people with the Quran and might appear upright, while in reality they are far from it. So, when you wish to seek treatment, it is essential that you ask trustworthy people of the Sunnah about those who use legitimate Islamic treatments and do not simply ask random people.

ADVICE FOR WOMEN

Know that women suffer from the majority of incidents of Evil Eye or envy, so make sure to do the following:

1) Gain knowledge of your religion in order to be acquainted with the commands of legislation and seek forgiveness a great deal, for what afflicts women does not happens except due to sins and disobedience.

2) Do not go out often except out of need and do so without displaying beauty. For truly, Satan raises his stare towards any woman who leaves her home and he makes her fair-seeming. This is among the reasons for being afflicted with Evil Eye.

3) Wear the legally-defined veil which covers the entire body and stay far away from: fashionable veils that are thin which define the body like a gown; colors which attract attention; decorative embroideries; and any transparent fabrics- none of these can be considered "veils", so do not deceive yourselves.

4) Beware of dresses hemmed too high [above the ankle] and going out with perfume on. The chosen one [al-Muṣṭafā] ﷺ warned against all of that and it is from among the reasons for being afflicted.

5) Beware of going to parties like weddings and the like that have prohibited singing. This is due to the great number of evil people and demons who attend these events. They are the most malicious people in terms of envy.

6) Fear Allah regarding your veil and clothing even among other women and do not be misled by those who uncover themselves to the middle of their thighs, half of their chests and most of their backs with these lewd dresses. All of this exists in our societies and our parties specifically. Affliction with Evil Eye results from all of this.

7) Stay far away from prohibited gatherings of women- gatherings of gossip, slander, sarcasm and dishonor. Envy and unpraiseworthy competition grow in these types of gatherings.

8) Hold your tongue and keep secret the private matters of your home life from those close to you even more so than distant relations, for how many families have been afflicted due to this. Lower your voice among men and do not soften it, for someone

who has a disease in his heart might be enticed.

9) Commit yourself to regular Ruqyah treatment from Evil Eye and envy and utilize oil and water that has been recited over as a drink or to rub with.

10) Beware of extravagance, squandering, pride, and excess for appearances in front of people.

11) Guard the five prayers, regularly preferred actions of the Prophet and the midnight prayer specifically- for the Divine Descent occurs in it and supplications are responded to. So, perform the midnight prayer with concentration.

12) Supplicate to Allah constantly while you are certain of the response after purifying what you eat, for if it is from what is prohibited, then Allah will not respond to you. Choose the best time for a response to your supplications and do not seek to rush a response from Allah, for it is said in a narration: "You will receive a response as long as you do not rush, thus, someone might say, "I have supplicated to my Lord and He has not responded to me"." *Ṣaḥīḥ Muslim #6870*

13) Perhaps you might dislike something and it is better for you! Know that a calamity does not come in order to destroy and kill you, it only comes in

order to test your patience and try you.

ADVICE FOR MEN

1) Gain knowledge regarding your religion for truly the first question in front of Allah will be about your family.

2) Raise your family based on goodwill by means of equal distribution and persuasion; and be an example for them.

3) Beware of pride and competing with your brothers that they might envy you.

4) Resort to keeping private the successes in all of your affairs.

5) Restrain your tongue and do not expose three things: age and wealth as much as you can and beliefs, for over these three things, you will be tested with another three- a falsifier, a cheat and deceiver.

6) Beware of evil companions who, when they leave, bite their fingertips over you out of rage.

7) You must protect yourself and your household.

8) Give voluntary charity frequently and persist in doing so.

TOOLS UTILIZED AS ORNAMENTS FALSELY BELIEVING THAT THEY REPEL EVIL EYE & ENVY

They are among the mistaken beliefs and things which lead to polytheism and refuge is sought in Allah:

- **The Blue Eye:** It is worn in necklaces and bracelets; it is common among young women and older women and its goal is to repel Evil Eye and envy.

- **The Five and the Talisman:** Some have written on them Quranic verses in order to cast a shadow over people [obscure the matt er for them]. There is a legal verdict on the lack of permissibility to hang them and even if they contain the Quran, they have the same ruling.

- The Belief that sending blessings on the Prophet repels the Evil Eye.

- Naming children with ugly names believing that it will repel the Evil Eye from them.

- Breaking eggs on a vehicle and similar things.

- Belief in placing Quranic verses made out of gold, silver or similar materials on the chests of infants- it is an insult to the Book of Allah, lofty and exalted is He, due to the lack of ability for infants to understand the meaning and importance of those verses.

- Belief that certain amulets containing black seed, barley, money, salt, morning glory, or other seeds will repel Evil Eye and envy.

- It is not permissible to burn herbs as incense believing that they will heal Evil Eye or that they are a repellant for sorcerers/witches. There is no harm in utilizing herbs as a functional supplement in areas where there is a proven benefit, however it must be without believing in it [as a treatment for Evil Eye and envy].

LEGAL VERDICT [FATWĀ] ABOUT AROMATHERAPY

Question: Shaykh Bin Bāz, may Allah have mercy on him, was asked there are some reciters [of Ruqyah] who describe remedies that are sold by perfume and oil sellers. They are placed on coals then the sick person burns it as incense and its smoke fills the rooms of the house like morning glory and similar herbs. [What about this?]

Answer: When there is a benefit, there is no harm in the majority of remedies [verified] by testing. When things are found to benefit people through testing [them] such as incense, rubbing oil, drinks, etc.- and found to have benefits- there is no harm in such remedies. It is not a *Tawqīfī* matt er, i.e. something derived from revelation wherein reason is suspended, rather it is utilized under the condition that it is not impure or prohibited by Islamic law. Thus, it is something whose use is permissible, like permissible seeds or other things which are not legally warned against.

Shaykh ʿAbd al-ʿAzīz bin Bāz

ALSO AVAILABLE BY LIGHT PUBLISHING

ALSO AVAILABLE BY LIGHT PUBLISHING

www.ingramcontent.com/pod-product-compliance
Lightning Source LLC
Chambersburg PA
CBHW012009090526
44590CB00026B/3943